Christiane Santos Haidar

The Influence of Hans Jonas' Principle of Responsibility

Christiane Santos Haidar

The Influence of Hans Jonas' Principle of Responsibility

Education, politics and economics

ScienciaScripts

SUMMARY

SUMMARY

Hans Jonas was a German philosopher who lived through the horrors of the Second World War. This experience led him to question the way man uses scientific knowledge and technology. His first writings were about *gnosis,* but in the 1970s he turned his attention to the human-technology-biosphere relationship. From this period onwards, Jonas began his philosophical analysis, which culminated in 'The Principle of Responsibility, an essay on ethics for technological civilization' (1979). In this work, Hans Jonas addresses three main themes: the critique of traditional ethics, the use of technology and scientific knowledge, and the heuristic of fear. The discussion presents the principle of responsibility in the form of a new imperative: 'act in such a way that the effects of your action are compatible with the permanence of authentic human life on Earth'. The global environmental crisis, unbridled consumption and the indiscriminate exploitation of natural resources make Jonah's presuppositions relevant and topical, so that they are recognized in areas such as education, politics and economics. In this work we have tried to identify the influence and importance of Jonasian thought in the areas mentioned, with the aim of highlighting the urgency of building new behaviors (in individual actions) and new paradigms (in collective actions), so that the biosphere is treated with dignity, and so that those to come have the right to enjoy it as the current generation does.

KEY WORDS

Ethics, Hans Jonas, environment, responsibility, technoscience.

1. INTRODUCTION

Hans Jonas (1903-1993) is considered to be the last of the Jewish philosophers born in Germany. He experienced the various crises that occurred throughout the 20th century, such as the two great wars, the advent of Nazism and technological advances. This traumatic experience led him to analyze the way in which humanity views nature, especially in terms of the use of technology combined with science.

Although Hans Jonas began his intellectual and philosophical career with an *'investigation into gnosis, in the 1970s he turned to problems related to ethics and technical-scientific development'* (1) (p.134).

The results of any action have future repercussions, so science and technology are not neutral, and can involve different intentions and possibilities during their use. This was the main point of analysis in Jonah's thinking, and it has repercussions in various areas of philosophy (2).

In his main writing on ethics, The Principle of Responsibility: an essay in ethics for technological civilization (PR) (3), Jonas proposes a new content for ethics and a new meaning for what we call responsibility. *'At the basis of his proposal are three fundamental points: 1) the critique of traditional ethics; 2) the use of technology; and 3) the heuristic of fear'* (1) (p.131).

Hans Jonas evaluated how classical ethics would deal with the problems related to the use of modern technology and concluded that the object of that science was limited to addressing the problem of men and their interactions with each other. With this conclusion, Jonas characterizes traditional ethics as strictly anthropocentric, and therefore inefficient for addressing contemporary problems about the use of technoscience, and humanity's relationship with non-human beings and the environment (1).

The German philosopher considered that current generations have the commitment to make the continuity of life and the survival of future generations possible, but to do so, it is necessary to review the power of science. *'Because of the importance of technoscience, and particularly technoscientific research and development, in shaping the future of the planet, the elaboration of a technoscientific ethic is one of the crucial issues of our time'* (4) (p.326).

As a third presupposition for the construction of this new ethic, Jonas states that moral philosophy should consult our fears rather than our desires, in the sense that *'fear would be the way to curb the Promethean compulsion and omnipotence to consider scientific knowledge unlimited'* (5) (p.77).

The essence of technology is built on the thinking of Francis Bacon (1561-1626), who is considered to be the founder of modern science, and responsible for the idea that scientific knowledge was intended to serve man and give him the power to conquer and subjugate the course of nature. This concept led humanity to use natural resources in a way that disrespected their carrying capacity, and to consider non-human animals as beings of only instrumental value.

Nowadays, we can see that science is increasing the power of technology, which brings fabulous promises but also threats of destruction and servitude, and, in one way or another, human beings are becoming aware that their world has a tendency to fall apart (6,7).

Concern about the human-biosphere relationship is present in the philosophical, scientific, political and educational spheres, among others, as humanity admits every day that it needs to adopt a new stance if it is to remain on Earth. This analysis arises from the awareness of the extreme vulnerability of nature and the complexity of man's technological intervention, which demands the need to rethink the ethical principles of this relationship and to observe the assumptions of responsibility (5).

In this follow-up, the proposal for an ethic for a technological civilization, based on the principle of responsibility, according to Hans Jonas, is shared by authors and thinkers who are also opinion formers, contributing to the construction of new pedagogical, political and economic values for the ordinary citizen.

We consider Hans Jonas' principle of responsibility to be an indispensable element for analyzing and restructuring the human relationship with the biosphere of which it is a part, since this presupposition offers subsidies for rethinking human dignity and nature on a new basis. Based on this assumption, this work aims to evaluate the relevance of

Hans Jonas' PR for the construction of a new understanding of human action (especially involving technoscience), as well as identifying the influence of Jonasian thought on other areas, such as politics, economics and education.

2. LITERATURE REVIEW

2.1 THE WORK OF HANS JONAS

Hans Jonas was born in 1903 in Mochengladbach, Germany. He studied philosophy and theology in Freiburg, Berlin and Heidelberg. He was a student of Martin Heidegger (considered by many to be Germany's greatest philosopher of the 20th century) and Rudolf Bultmann (one of Germany's most famous reformist theologians). During his doctorate he met the philosopher Hannah Arendt, with whom he maintained a long friendship and shared similar ideologies. He fought in the Jewish Brigade of the British Army and lived in Canada and the United States of America, where he taught at important universities. He died in 1993 in New York (8, 3, 1).

Since the 1950s, the German philosopher has paid special attention to the theme of nature in his works, and has not failed to address the subject in interviews and articles produced throughout his academic life. In the early 1970s, Hans Jonas published several texts that contained the germ of his ideas on the use of technology and its consequences, some of which were brought together in the collection Technique, Medicine and Ethics, published in 1985 (9). In this collection, Jonas states that because technology interferes in everything that relates to human beings, and because it has become a problem that threatens human existence on Earth, the need has arisen to create a philosophy for technology (1).

Continuing his discussions on the relationship between man and nature, during the 1980s until his death, Hans Jonas gave several interviews on environmental issues. Nine of them were collected and published in Germany under the title *Dem bosen Ende naher,* in 1993, and with a subsequent French publication. In one of these interviews, Jonas assessed the environmental crisis as the set of consequences of anthropic action, such as *'overpopulation, disturbance of the natural balance and extinction of species'* (9) (p.471). He also stated that there was an urgent need to define new values and strategies, new forms of expression and governance that would protect man from the inconstancy of his collective action, which deprives nature of its own self-regulating mechanisms (10).

But it was in 1979 that his main work was published. The book Principle of Responsibility, an essay on ethics for technological civilization (PR) was written in the philosopher's mother tongue, German, and was only translated into English in 1984. Since its publication, PR has become a reference for countless discussions on human action involving techno-scientific knowledge, reaching spheres beyond the philosophical circuits.

The writer Rachel Salamander, in the prologue to Hans Jonas' Memorias, pointed out that:

No book by an academic philosopher in the German-speaking twentieth century was as quickly and widely distributed as PR. The philosopher suddenly achieved great popularity, becoming a sought-after media figure and a major presence at conferences and debates on ecological problems and the future of the planet (1) (p.131).

The relevance of Hans Jonas' thinking has earned him several awards and prizes, including the German Publishers' Peace Prize in 1987 and the title of *Honorary Doctor of* Philosophy awarded by the *Freie Universitat Berlin in* 1992, a year before his death (10).

Several contemporary scholars consider that Jonas has become a reference point for the field of education and applied ethics, as well as philosophy, challenging pertinent questions about how to educate for life in a contemporary technological society (5,10). The book The Principle of Responsibility is divided into six chapters, in which the author analyzes classical and modern ethics, seeking to demonstrate how they are unable to deal with possibility or the future, but only with proximity and the present. He expresses deep concern about the problems of our time and seeks to formulate a new ethical principle, or to put it another way, a new imperative for morality, because, according to him, these problems are of such complexity and magnitude that they can no longer be tackled in the light of traditional ethics. The thinker mainly criticizes

Aristotelian and Kantian ethics (8,1).

Chapter I - The changed nature of human action - analyzes the different perspectives of classical ethics, in an attempt to demonstrate that it is no longer capable of dealing with the new challenges of human action, given that modern technology has introduced axes of unprecedented magnitude, with new objects and consequences. It also identifies the subjugation of *Homo sapiens* by *Homo faber,* because for every step in the development of technology, new needs arise, which demand new processes, building an uninterrupted chain that is increasingly autonomous.

Still in the first chapter, Jonas questions the Kantian imperative, considering it inadequate or incomplete for today, and proposes a new imperative: *'Act in such a way that the effects of your action are compatible with the permanence of authentic human life on Earth'* (3) (p.47).

Chapter II - Questions of Principle and Method - develops the project in five topics on the need for a non-reciprocal principle of responsibility, with regard to future generations and planetary life. In this chapter, Jonas also presents the concept of the 'heuristic of fear', which can be translated as the need to consult our fears rather than our desires when applying technology, in other words, we must act with caution.

In Chapter III - On ends and their position in being - the German thinker constructs a critical ontological-ethical perspective on the concepts of good, value, life, survival, fear, proximity and the future. Jonas believes that everything has its own purpose: human beings, animals, plants and the biosphere itself. E,

regardless of their function, their purpose is to participate in the natural cycle of life.

In chapter IV - The good, the duty and the being, a theory of responsibility - Jonas recovers and develops the idea introduced in chapter II about the perspective of an ethic of responsibility, based on caring for future generations and the biosphere, permeating politics, religion and moral values.

The fifth and sixth chapters explain what the new PR ethic would look like, and develop *'a critique of utopia, especially political utopias which, while denying the present, beckon of paradisiacal futures sustained by technological potential'* (10).

(p.15). In these chapters, the philosopher basically analyzes the political and economic models in force at the time: capitalism and socialism.

Chapter V - Responsibility today: the threatened future and the idea of progress - analyzes the contemporary concept of progress, technological and scientific advances, capitalism *versus* Marxism as two ways of dealing with the problems arising from technological and scientific advances, and the utopias that drive these two political conceptions. The author notes that none of the systems that divided and governed the world at the time served their purpose, for different reasons, ending up defending the ethical-political power of specialists, with broad authority to subject collective action to the demands of the imperative of responsibility.

In Chapter VI - The Critique of Utopia and the Ethics of Responsibility - Jonas continues his rejection of political-economic systems, defending the need for the principle of responsibility. He states that:

The ethic of responsibility, which today, after several centuries of post-Baconian and Promethean euphoria, from which Marxism also originated, must hold back the reins of this galloping progress. Restraining such progress should be seen as nothing more than an intelligent precaution, accompanied by simple decency towards our descendants (3) (p.349).

Fernandes identifies five stages of the human-nature relationship, which are addressed in Jonas' work: *"dominance, ambivalence, decentering, holism and the principle of responsibility"* (10) (p.21). Domination refers to the period of the modern era, in which man no longer reveres nature but submits it to human design. In this phase Hans Jonas warns that *'the scientific view of nature refuses us any theoretical right to think of nature as something we should respect, since it has reduced it to the indifference of necessity and chance, stripping it of all dignity of ends'* (3) (p.41).

With regard to ambivalence, modern man was successful in his techno-scientific endeavors, but contemporary man suffers from various negative impacts, such as climate instability, the depletion of natural resources and social exclusion. Here, Jonas states that *'The threat of catastrophe to the Baconian ideal of the domination of nature by means of technology lies, therefore, in the magnitude of its success'* (3) (p.235).

In the stage of decentralization, man becomes aware of the risks he is running in the worst way, since 'the realization that *the acceleration of technologically-fueled development reduces our time for self-corrections, that is, they are increasingly difficult and the freedom to carry them out is ever smaller'* (3) (p.78-79). This new vision compels him to overcome the utilitarian paradigm that has dominated thinking in recent centuries.

In the holistic phase, nature is seen as a totality, and the arrogant attitude gives way to respect and conscious self-limitation. *In* this line of thought, PR states that *'From a truly human perspective, nature retains its dignity, which stands in contrast to the arbitrariness of our power. Insofar as she has generated us, we owe allegiance to the totality of her creation'* (3) (p.229).

In the last stage, the responsibility principle states that there are limits to the consumer society, given that *"an entirely new object, no less than the entire biosphere of the planet, has been added for which we must be responsible, because we have power over it"* (3) (p.39).

In this way, Hans Jonas very pertinently addressed the need for a new ethical outlook on human actions in the technological age, which would culminate in the creation of new behaviors, based on the principle of non-reciprocal responsibility towards future generations and the biosphere. This responsibility was considered by Jonas to be intrinsic to man, since only the human species possesses clarity of thought, understanding and the ability to choose between various possible paths.

2.2 PERCEPTION OF THE ENVIRONMENT

We can say that the awakening to the environmental crisis came after the Second World War, because the event made it clear that technological development does not go hand in hand with moral evolution. The questionable human behavior that was demonstrated at that time in inter-individual relations, with total contempt for certain groups of people, is also revealed in the human-biosphere relationship, when man assumes that nature has no value in itself, only to serve his interests.

Discussions about the environment have occupied a central position in contemporary society and are a reflection of the ethical and moral crisis plaguing various sectors that directly affect people, such as health, economics and politics. This concern is due to the fact that anthropic action and civilization itself have an impact on the environment from the local spatial scale to the planetary scale, in such a disturbing way that it can be compared to destabilizing geological forces, capable of interfering with the biological cycles of animals and plants and even the climate (11, 12, 13).

And in this increasingly globalized world, the future has been perceived in a contradictory way: as progress by those who consider a supposed integrating power, especially of the economic and material kind; and as a place of catastrophe by others, due to ecological crises and the progressive depletion of finite and scarce resources to sustain the civilizing process (13) (p.71).

Regarding the globalization of environmental problems, Jonas already pointed out that *'the warning blows that tormented nature sends us know no territorial boundaries'* (9) (p.476).

With the need to build a new perception of the importance of the environment, various philosophical and scientific sectors have begun to turn their attention to environmental problems in order not only to resolve existing aggressions, but also with the aim of getting to know the biosphere, understanding it in order to protect it. In other words, a movement began to practice the principle of responsibility, as preached by Hans Jonas. This movement is reflected in the emergence of environmental sciences, such as ecology and environmental ethics, which aim to understand the natural environment and the relationships between its biotic and abiotic components. These sciences involve more than simply collecting data and understanding scientific issues on a specific subject, but are also linked to value systems and questions of social justice (12).

Botkin and Keller attribute values to the environment through various justifications, including moral justification. According to the authors, this justification is related to the *'conviction that the natural environment has a right to exist, and that human beings have a moral obligation to allow it to continue to exist'* (12) (p.14). The analysis of environmental values is the focus of environmental ethics, which also deals with the commitment to future generations. In this context, we can ask: *'should we have a moral obligation to leave the environment in good condition for those yet to come, or do we have complete freedom to use environmental resources to the point of complete exhaustion for the duration of our lives?'* (12) (p.14). In response to this question, Hans Jonas states that: *'my action cannot jeopardize the total interest of all others also involved (which are, here, the interests of future generations'* (3) (p.85).

Human awakening to the importance of the biosphere has reached more and more segments, and since the middle of the last century, *'the tendency to conceive of the planet as a homeland and humanity as a people inhabiting a common home'* (2) (p.51) has been *consolidated.* These ideas are shared by important writers, such as Arendt and Morin, who claim that it is necessary to build a concept of planetary citizenship (Morin) or a common homeland (Arendt), in which human activities would consider the entire globe as the recipient of their actions, and that each individual would have a shared responsibility for the entire planet. Morin states that *"it is necessary to register the complex planetary crisis that marked the 20th century, showing that all human beings, confronted from now on with the same problems of life and death, share a common destiny"* (14) (p.16), since we are living beings on this planet, we depend vitally on the earth's biosphere, and we must therefore recognize our earthly, physical and biological identity.

The concept of planetary citizenship is identified by Fernandes in Jonah's work and is considered to be close to Aristotelian ideas. *'In Aristotle's thought, man, as a natural and rational being, endowed with freedom and responsibility, is obliged to watch over the order of the universe, the entire biosphere, since the balance of the natural order is precarious'* f10) (p.125). On the other hand, Jonas recognizes that Aristotle could never have imagined that man would become so harmful to the planet, because for the

Greek *'human reason, thanks to which man stood out in nature, would be incapable of harming that same nature by its contemplation'* (3) (p.231). Such thinking proved to be a mistake as soon as man left contemplation to intervene and modify nature.

Concerns about the human-nature relationship are also present in religious circles. Their representatives reflect on the ideas of thinkers, philosophers, scientists, theologians and social organizations that deal with the subject, and insert them into the documents addressed to their followers.

In 1971, Pope Paul VI referred to the ecological problem as a dramatic consequence of human activities, which risk destroying nature and also falling victim to this degradation. The Catholic High Priest also addressed the FAO, which is the United Nations branch responsible for matters related to agriculture and food, when he warned of a possible ecological catastrophe under the effect of the explosion of industrial civilization, stressing the urgent need for a radical change in humanity's behavior. He considered that *'the most extraordinary scientific progress, the most astonishing technical inventions, the most prodigious technical development, if they are not united with social and moral progress, necessarily turn against man'* (2) (p.2).

Pope Francis, in his 2015 encyclical, *Laudato Si, spells* out several points that need to be re-evaluated in this relationship, giving relevance to the issue and calling on governments and Catholics to reflect on the construction of public policies and on individual behavior and its consequences (13). For the Pontiff, the concept of integral ecology is inseparable from the notion of the common good. Pope Francis considers the challenge of protecting our common home to be urgent. This protection would include the *'concern to unite the entire human family in the search for sustainable and integral development'* (2) (p.5), because planetary changes are notorious.

Patriarch Bartholomew of the Orthodox Church referred *'particularly to the need for everyone to repent of their own mistreatment of the planet, because everyone, to the extent that we cause minor ecological damage, is called to recognize our contribution to the disfigurement of the environment'* (2) (p.3). It also invites people to find solutions not only in technology, but also in behavioral change, otherwise only the symptoms would be addressed

Also reporting a spiritual aspect of the responsibility of human action, Capra differentiates shallow ecology (anthropocentric) from deep ecology (founded by the Norwegian philosopher Arne Naess), considering the latter as a spiritual or religious consciousness. The physicist understands that:

When the concept of the human spirit is understood as the mode of consciousness in which the individual feels connected to the cosmos as a whole, it becomes clear that ecological consciousness is spiritual in its deepest essence, and is compatible with the perennial philosophy of spiritual traditions (15) (p.20-21).

This idea is shared by theologian Leonardo Boff when he says that *'we have to be sensitive to each other, cooperative in all our activities, respectful of other beings in nature, in other words, we have to be spiritual'* (16) (p.43).

From the point of view of environmental sciences and applied ethics, a path is emerging to combine knowledge and build new paradigms, since ecological concepts and their models are being used in various fields and are gaining importance in various areas of knowledge (17).

2.3 THE PRINCIPLE OF RESPONSIBILITY ACCORDING TO PHILOSOPHY, ETHICS AND BIOETHICS

The contemporary individual not only has great freedom and the power to act, which has been expanded and transformed by technical and scientific advances, but is also faced with significantly greater dilemmas and responsibilities than ever before' (4) (p.325-326). It is this enhanced spectrum of human action that opens up space for a new range of questions and problems, which in turn require a re-dimensioning of ethical reflection, inserting an already well-known concept into the center of the debate, but one that has never been so closely associated with this development: the question of responsibility (1).

It is well known that *'all knowledge carries the risk of error and illusion'* (14) (p.19), and that these have populated the human mind since the emergence of *Homo sapiens.* Hannah Arendt had already questioned whether *'one of the attributes of the activity of thinking, in its intrinsic nature, is the possibility of preventing evil from being done'* (18) (p.393). By posing this question, the philosopher demonstrated how deeply the relationship between thinking and acting should be analyzed. Hans Jonas amplifies this relevance when he recognizes that every action carries with it consequences that must be calculated or foreseen.

In this field of discussion, philosophy, which is by nature a reflection on any human problem, becomes a field closed in on itself when, in analyzing specific, anthropocentric situations, it leaves out the collaboration of the sciences. Such compartmentalization weakens global perception, which in turn weakens responsibility, as well as loosening the lakes of solidarity, in the sense that each individual does not feel the links with their fellow citizens. (14). This was Jonah's main criticism of classical ethics, as he no longer considered it sufficient to deal with the new technological era, which, as well as being highly transformative of the natural environment, also altered human action itself.

But despite all this behavioral transformation resulting from the power conferred by technology, it is undeniable that responsibility is an essentially human prerogative, even if the megalomaniac idea of dominion over the world has sometimes been disseminated, leading us to believe that caring for nature and non-human beings would be the service of the weak. In this way, the correct interpretation of the concept of human beings is to understand them as responsible stewards of our common home, planet Earth (2).

Nowadays, different perspectives and lines of thought have developed on the relationship between man and nature and non-human beings. At one extreme, some defend the myth of progress, claiming that ecological problems will simply be solved with new technical applications, without ethical considerations or paradigm shifts. At the other extreme, others believe that human intervention can only threaten and jeopardize the world's ecosystem, which would justify reducing their presence on the planet and even preaching zero population growth (7). Between these extremes, reflection should identify possible future scenarios, because there isn't just one path to a solution. Therefore, *'the attitudes that hinder the solution range from denial of the problem to indifference, complacent resignation or blind trust in technical solutions'* (2) (p.5).

Several contemporary authors also share Jonah's opinion when they emphasize that ethics should not only refer to man, but should extend its gaze to the biosphere as a whole, seeking a global and transcendental vision, associating philosophical and scientific knowledge (5, 19). This association is justified because ethics now has to do with agendas and no longer with isolated subjects.

Applied ethics emerged in the 1960s and 1970s as a new form of analysis, pluralistic and more comprehensive than the morality of everyday life and the ethics of classical philosophy (20). In this context, global ethics is understood as *'the systematic study of human behavior in the life and health sciences examined in the light of moral values and principles'* (21) (p.46), an analysis that Hans Jonas has always preached as indispensable for the techno-scientific era that man was entering. This new approach led to the creation of Bioethics, a term coined by Fritz Jahr and quoted in articles published between 1927 and 1947, which was revived by Van Rensselaer Potter, who popularized it and expanded its field of study (22).

Lecaros states that Potter's proposal came about to face the new challenges arising from techno-scientific development, in other words, he set out to create an ethical discipline that would be received as a realistic and inseparable understanding of human actions with the environment. For the scholar, Jahr and Potter's global bioethics scheme has its philosophical foundation in three ideas: the principle of responsibility, the pluralism of values and planetary citizenship (22).

The construction of Potter's bioethics takes into account the knowledge of the biological and environmental sciences of his time, which was already being disseminated with the reports of the environmental crisis in books such as Raquel Carson's Silent Spring. In this way, we cannot detach Potter's proposal for global bioethics from Hans Jonas' ethics of responsibility (22). In Bioethics, a bridge to the future, Potter lists seven points necessary for building an ideal environment for humanity. Among these, we highlight the *'demand for a culture that respects the solid principles of ecology as a far-reaching point of view. The purpose must be to live with nature as in a balanced aquarium, without assumptions about the ability of future science to rescue a sick planet'* (7) (p.162). In this follow-up, Hans Jonas also questioned whether science really had solutions for all the problems that would arise in relation to human permanence on Earth, or whether, on the other hand, it wouldn't be better to build behaviors based on precaution.

2.4 THE USE OF TECHNIQUE, DANGEROUS KNOWLEDGE AND THE HEURISTICS OF FEAR

The systematic use of the most modern technologies available at the time of Hitler made science suspect of being capable of what was most feared: the possibility of the systematic destruction of life on previously unimaginable scales (8). It was against this backdrop of war that Hans Jonas concluded that humanity needed to devise new ways of acting, given that *'the promise of modern technology has become a threat, or has become indissolubly associated with it'* (3) (p.21). The 20th century revealed that human evolution came hand in hand with the power of death. This death is not only that resulting from two world wars and their thousands of corpses, but also from two other increasingly real dangers. The first is the possibility of the global extinction of all humanity by nuclear weapons. The second is the possibility of ecological death. Since the 1970s, we have discovered that the waste, emanations and exhalations of urban technical-industrial development are degrading the biosphere and threatening to irreparably poison the environment in which we live. In other words, *'the unbridled domination of nature by technology is leading humanity to suicide'* (14) (p.71).

The events mentioned led humanity to know the worst about itself, and revealed that *'science is knowledge, but it is not wisdom. Wisdom is the knowledge of how to use science and how to balance it with other knowledge'* (7) (p.70). The concept of prudence is a criterion of moderation for human life and also for the use of techno-scientific knowledge, because not everything you can do, you should do. Both prudence and precaution reflect the idea of Hans Jonas' heuristic of fear, which is at the service of the ethics of the future, since it makes man aware of the limits of his knowledge, instilling in him a sense of uncertainty about the future, and at the same time prescribing that on a practical level it is always better to give priority to the bad prognosis rather than the good one, in order to avoid the greater evils that can arise from the dynamic and cumulative effect of technology (10).

But on the good or bad characteristic of scientific knowledge, Jonas stated that *'like any faculty or capacity of human beings, technology is not in itself good or bad. In Jonas' view, any human capacity is, in principle, a good thing; it is only its misuse that generates negative and harmful consequences for the human being himself'* (1) (p.136). Thus, it is because of the indiscriminate use of scientific knowledge and technology that the ethics of responsibility must make fear its first word, but it is that fear that prompts precaution, care, not unfounded and paralyzing fear (9).

In the same vein that inspires caution, one of the dilemmas of modern society is the phenomenon of dangerous knowledge. No one has ever possessed the omniscience to foresee all the implications of new knowledge and its possible misapplications. Dangerous knowledge is often not recognized as such at the time of its discovery. It can be defined as knowledge that has accumulated faster than the wisdom to

to manage it. Another point that enhances the threat of dangerous knowledge is the fact that many scientists violently fight the idea of its existence, arguing that any increase in knowledge is beneficial in itself (7). In this regard, Potter considers the responsible nature of most scientists to the detriment of political aloofness when he states:

It is now clear that the rapid pace of development in science and technology will continue and that our national and international policies must deal with both the possibilities and the dangers of the revolution that has taken place in the ways of knowing and doing. Society must pay more attention to the far-reaching consequences of our daily government decisions. I believe that most scientists would see the peaceful preservation of our terrestrial environment and the balance between population and environment as high priority goals for the future (7) (p.100).

Another form in which we find the concept of dangerous knowledge in philosophy of science texts is that of the *slippery slope.* The term tells us that *'if something is possible, human beings will do it, whether it's good or bad, right or wrong, and although what is immediately being proposed may be correct, it is not.*

will inevitably lead to the worst, until you reach the bottom of the slope where there are unknown horrors' (23) (p.84). The slippery slope and
often cited in works on genetic manipulation, which is a very broad part of science (covering cloning to the creation of genetically modified organisms), and which is developing rapidly.

2.5   MODERN BIOTECHNOLOGY AND THE RESPONSIBILITY

Science is the search for an understanding of nature and the physical material world, while technology is the application of scientific knowledge. Science usually leads to technological development, just as new technologies contribute to scientific discoveries (12).

But while in the past, science could be seen as a source of material well-being and as the organizer and holder of little knowledge, it is now perceived by many as the source of considerable disorder and knowledge that society is not prepared to manage by any means (7) (p.84).

The 20th century produced gigantic advances in all areas of scientific knowledge, as well as in all fields of technology, but at the same time it produced a new blindness to global, fundamental and complex problems, and this blindness has generated countless mistakes and illusions, starting with scientists, technicians and specialists, as humanity seems to be getting more and more involved in experiments to destroy itself and its world (24, 14).

Pope Francis points out that today we have the best technical and scientific conditions in our history, but he warns us that these conditions cannot be understood as if they were neutral, as they cause other problems, including the technocratic paradigm, in which man, reduced to a mere object of technology, closes in on himself and thinks of his existence as independent from the totality of life. Morin agrees with the High Priest's concern and states that the 21st century is a time of uncertainty, with an urgent need to re-evaluate the consequences of scientific discoveries and use (14, 25).

As technology has taken us from being subjects dominated by nature to being masters of nature, Hans Jonas' question becomes absolutely topical: isn't it time to reflect on how we act with the responsibility that this power has brought us, towards future generations and the environment? In the same vein, in her introduction to Silent Spring, Linda Lear states that the writer Raquel Carson feared that technology was advancing faster than humanity's sense of moral responsibility. In this work, Carson denounces the consequences of the large-scale use of organochlorine and organophosphate insecticides on organisms that were not the object of the spraying and on the natural environment. The report was responsible for countless discussions on the subject, culminating in the banning of some biocides (organic-persistent pollutants) in several countries with the Stockholm Treaty in 1972 (24). It was with this analysis of the power conferred on man by technology that Jonas concluded that *Homo faber* overlapped with *Homo sapiens*. This thought is echoed in Hannah Arendt's writings when she recognizes the existence of *'a problematic equation of intelligence with ingenuity, to which humanity is heir without the right of return'* (1) (p.137).

On the other hand, contrary to Jonasian thinking, some scientists, such as Mary Warnock, argue that:

Since human beings, and only human beings, have the ability to come close to understanding the universe, including themselves, by scientific methods, they have a duty to do so. There is nothing to be said for trying to stop the search for knowledge at any point, even if it were possible (23) (p.74).

Beyond this proposition, according to Azambuja, the Jonahian concern about the consequences of the use of technoscience no longer has a place, in the sense that:

Contemporary techno-science is different from modern technology in that its aim is not to extract and exploit natural resources. On the other hand, it has as one of its fundamental goals the manipulation and creation of artificial forms of life, whether human, technological or environmental, based on the manipulation of nature's elementary data (4) (p.324).

2.6   THE INFLUENCE OF JONASIAN THOUGHT ON LAW, POLITICS AND ECONOMICS

Morin identifies two major ethical-political goals for the current millennium: *'to establish a relationship of mutual control between society and individuals through democracy and to conceive of humanity as a planetary community'* (14) (p.17-18). The last goal proposed by the French educator mirrors Hans Jonas' ideal in the sense that the philosopher recognized the need for human beings to act consciously and responsibly. This responsibility would also be linked to public man, in the construction of public policies that would protect future generations and the natural environment.

The principle of responsibility and the heuristic of fear are clearly recognizable in the modern foundations of areas of law and have given rise to relevant guidance for government action. The precautionary principle was enshrined in international environmental law with the mission of providing legislators and politicians with an instrument for international regulation of technological innovation and human activity in general. *'As a result, the precautionary principle (based on the ideas of Hans Jonas) is being extended to all decisions likely to cause risk' (*10) (p.129).

This principle stems from Principle 15 of the Rio-92 Conference, which states:

In order to protect the environment, the precautionary principle must be widely observed by states, according to their capacities. When there is a threat of serious or irreversible damage, the absence of absolute scientific certainty should not be used as a reason to postpone effective and economically viable measures to prevent environmental degradation (19) (p.106).

The Rio 92 Declaration contains 27 principles which seek to reconcile the rational, beneficial and legitimate use of natural resources with their conservation for the years to come. In its third principle, the Declaration states that *'the right to development must be exercised in such a way as to respond equitably to the environmental and development needs of present and future generations'* (21) (p.50). This principle explicitly presents the ideas of Jonah, in which the philosopher emphasized the concern for ethical behavior that would preserve the possibility of a dignified life for our descendants, present in the imperative he proposed.

In addition to these assumptions, which have been used to build legal instruments, in recent decades the concept of environmental justice has emerged as a necessary principle for evaluating geographical situations and guiding decision-making in environmental matters (21). This concept appears in Brazil's Federal Constitution, in Article 225, which states: *"Everyone has the right to an ecologically balanced environment, which is a good for the common use of the people and essential to a healthy quality of life, and the public authorities and the community have the duty to defend and preserve it for present and future generations"* (19) (p.64).

The precautionary principle is widely used in Brazilian environmental public policies. This legislation is recognized as one of the strictest and most protective in the world. In this respect, Hans Jonas' assumptions are emphatically followed, given that any action that compromises the natural environment demands compensation or makes it impossible to carry it out.

The reflections of the German philosopher are also present in economics, where some authors emphasize the need to re-evaluate the parameters used as economic indicators, suggesting expanding them to others with a qualitative focus. This tendency is in line with Shramm's thinking when he states that the dimension of economic development does not necessarily imply a corresponding and expected integral human development, which can be seen as a threat to human survival itself. In other words, economic development needs to involve quality of life parameters that are not only linked to financial *status* (13).

Also along these lines, in 1971 Potter predicted that:

Over the next three decades, we will witness a fateful dispute between two schools of thought. On one side will be the ecological conservationists, who emphasize two ideas: a) a commitment to maintaining a satisfactory life for human beings in the long-term future and b) the conviction that the first goal can only be achieved if technology does not cause violent and irreparable damage to the multitude of other organisms that maintain the organic variety of the total environment. On the other side of the dispute over the direction of public policy will be economists who are dismissive of biologists and assume that economic growth is not the only objective, but the only reliable test of technology (7) (p.179).

The change in economic paradigms began with the concept of sustainable development, created by the Brundtland Report during the World Commission on Environment and Development in 1983, developed by the United Nations (UN). The new concept proposed development that would meet present needs without compromising the ability of future generations to meet their own needs. Once again, this model recognizes the Jonahian imperative.

However, several scholars already consider sustainable development to be inadequate for the new social demands, and are proposing new concepts. Thus, faced with the challenge of overcoming the current model of sustainable development and preserving the dignity and continuity of human and non-human life in the future, the policy of degrowth emerges, with new paradigms. Its axis is aligned with the Jonahian proposal of responsibility.

Degrowth is a political-economic concept coined in the 1970s, partly based on the theses of Romanian economist Nicholas Georgescu-Roegen. This thesis is based on the hypothesis that economic growth (understood as a constant increase in Gross Domestic Product (GDP)) is not sustainable by the global ecosystem. The current model of production and consumption has no future, because it is leading us to self-extinction. The way out would be the adoption of new values and new customs, in short, the adoption of a new lifestyle (26).

Shramm classifies degrowth as:

An eco-anthropocentric convergence between concerns for the survival of the human species and, at the same time, some form of preservation of the environment in which it lives. This type of approach simultaneously recognizes: a) the rights of nature and its subsystems (animals, plants and ecosystems); b) the corresponding human duties (13) (p.72).

For economist Serge Latouche, the main issue regarding the economic-environmental problem is that natural resources are limited and therefore there is no such thing as infinite growth. Improving living conditions must therefore be achieved without increasing consumption, by changing the dominant paradigm. The economist also states that this is not a stationary state, nor is it a form of regression, recession or negative growth. The main point is the paradigm of unlimited growth. Degrowth also recognizes technology without the naivety of believing that its advance is proof that society should not free itself from consumerism. In this way, the ideology advocates activities that have less impact and a reduction in those that degrade the environment rapidly (27, 11, 13). Furthermore, degrowth should not be seen as a single alternative to the current model, but rather as a warning about the risks of the situation we live in, a cry for change. *'In this way, Hans Jonas' ethics for the future meets the Latouchian theory of degrowth, since it seeks to change the way of life in the present for the sake of future generations'* (11) (p.22).

2.7 THE RESPONSIBILITY OF EDUCATION IN BUILDING NEW PARADIGMS

Although Hans Jonas is not a thinker directly involved with the philosophy of education, his ideas are reflected in various pedagogical questions. Along these lines, Fernandes asks how PR could *'contribute to the emergence of a holistic educational paradigm that dethrones the anthropocentrism of the current dominant paradigm'* (10) (p.119). Education, being a human activity, presupposes the choice of a certain model of man and society, so, like science and technology, it is never neutral. However, even though Jonas is not considered a pillar of pedagogy, he recognizes that education is a relevant tool for building responsibility. In this regard, the philosopher states that education transforms the object of responsibility (the student) into the subject of responsibility (the citizen) (3).

Morin recognizes the importance of education for building planetary citizenship, translated into the conscious will to care (14). But the truth is that modern man has not been educated in the right use of power, because the immense technological growth has not been accompanied by the development of human beings in terms of responsibility, values and conscience (2). However,

In the countries that should be making the biggest changes in consumer habits, young people have a new ecological sensitivity and a generous spirit, and some of them are fighting admirably to defend the environment, despite having grown up in a context of high consumption and well-being that makes it difficult for other habits to mature. This is why we are facing an educational challenge (2) (p.64).

Along the same lines, Fernandes recognizes that *'the challenges facing contemporary education deserve a broad reflection that can be enriched in the light of Hans Jonas' thinking'* (10) (p.8). He goes on to ask whether

Wouldn't education for planetary citizenship be a valuable tool for preparing today's generation with the skills needed to face the threats ahead, given that school is the privileged place for formal learning and should be responsible for fostering values and developing attitudes (10) (p.31).

In Brazil, Law 9.795, of April 27, 1999, which provides for environmental education and establishes the National Environmental Education Policy, was the first governmental step to insert the discussion into all levels of education, and in a transversal way, that is, as a theme in all subjects. Environmental education is understood to be *'the processes through which individuals and the community build social values, knowledge, skills, attitudes and competences aimed at conserving the environment, which is a good for the common use of the people, essential to a healthy quality of life and its sustainability'* (19) (p.60-61). As we have already seen, sustainability or sustainable development has its foundations in the ideas of Hans Jonas, who advocates the preservation of a decent natural environment for future generations.

2.8 IS JONAHIAN THINKING TECHNOPHOBIC?

Several authors such as Gilbert Hottois, Marie Genevieve Pinsart and Dominique Lecourt classify Jonas as a technophobe (9, 4). To analyze this assessment, we have adopted the strict meaning of the term, according to its etymology, which is: morbid fear or aversion to technology.

Hottois identified three current philosophical perspectives on technoscience. He defined them as humanist technophobia, humanist technophilia and evolutionist technophilia. For the Belgian philosopher, technophobia warns of the dangers that civilization runs by trying to transgress the limits of nature (4).

Still addressing Hottois' analysis, he understands that Jonas poses two important problems for the use of technology: that of environmental destruction and that of the transformation of the essence of humanity, insofar as technological means threaten the global biosphere on the one hand, and on the other, threaten to modify, manipulate and transform the reality of human beings. He also warns that the imperative he proposes and his argument are nothing more than a *'philosophical illusion, because at every step, the presuppositions and definitions of the most important terms are filled with obscurities that can be contested'* (10) (p.96), insofar as they don't present evidence, nor the immediate universality he claims.

Fonseca argues that Jonasian thought does not accept the categorization of technophobe, quoting Jean Greisch, who points out that the heuristic of fear is *'one of the most criticized and misunderstood aspects of Hans Jonas' work'* (9) (p.475). However, Fonseca concludes in his work that Hans Jonas blames modern technology for the current environmental crisis, but points out that the philosopher also makes it clear that technology in itself is nothing more than a body of knowledge, and that the person responsible for applying it is man, who has power over it and is ultimately responsible for all the consequences of using it (9, 11).

From another point of view, Fernandes states that if we take Hans Jonas' thinking to its ultimate consequences, PR could point to:

a certain closure to the new, which would end up denying man freedom and the ability to create alternatives, and if we look at the past, it was this ability that distinguished him from the animal. Refusing man the freedom to face risk, to produce scenarios of possible paths, evoking the fear of catastrophe, seems rather limiting, given that facing risks and overcoming natural limitations has always been intrinsic to the human being (10) (p.145).

3. OBJECTIVES

3.1 GENERAL OBJECTIVE

Relate Hans Jonas' thought contained in the work 'The Responsibility Principle, an Essay on Ethics for Technological Civilization' to the thought of other contemporary philosophers and authors.

3.2 SPECIFIC OBJECTIVES

Identify the influence of Jonah's presuppositions in areas related to philosophy, such as education, economics and politics.

Analyze Hans Jonas' classification as a technophobic philosopher.

Evaluate the importance of the imperative proposed by Hans Jonas for the construction of new contemporary ethical-moral paradigms.

4. DISCUSSION

4.1 HANS JONAS' PROPOSITIONS AND THEIR RELEVANCE IN THE 21ST CENTURY

'An author's thought is not judged by its immediate use, but by the fertile seeds it sows and the questions it raises' (10) (p.119).

The development of scientific knowledge is a powerful means of detecting errors and combating illusions. However, the paradigms that control science can develop errors, and no scientific theory is immune to error. *'Furthermore, scientific knowledge cannot deal with epistemological, philosophical and ethical problems on its own'* (14) (p.71). In this way, since the use of technology is a human action, it becomes the object of ethics, but not of classical ethics, since many of the premises that limit human and existential issues, which were taken for granted in the anthropocentric conception, cannot be references for the contemporary model of life, since the old ethical precepts have lost their validity due to the change in human action. So, if on the one hand, classical ethics are still valid for dealing with certain problems, on the other hand, they are not sufficient or do not have the elements to analyze new challenges (1, 5).

Reflection on nature appears in Hans Jonas' earliest works (after his publications on *gnosis)*. Perhaps this is why the philosopher is among the group of thinkers who have revived the relevance of nature in philosophical questions (9). This importance is accentuated when we recognize that before Jonah's work, there was no talk of man's responsibility towards nature. This is because human action did not have as much power to intervene as it does in modern times and today.

Discussions about the use of technology and its consequences are the main theme of 'The Principle of Responsibility - an essay on ethics for technological civilization', a book that is still considered one of the most relevant on the subject. He draws attention to ethical problems that have arisen with the 20th and 21st centuries: the threat to the future of humanity and the violation of the integrity of human beings and nature caused by the unconditional commitment to the modern ideal of progress. The book is based on two fundamental criticisms: traditional ethics and the indiscriminate use of technology. The latter is related to Francis Bacon's idea of *'the domination of nature, which, operated progressively and exclusively by means of technology, constitutes for Hans Jonas the imminent threat of the annihilation of the human being"* (1) (p.138).

The German philosopher also presents the concept of the heuristic of fear, which advocates inserting precaution into all human actions, especially those involving technoscience. Finally, Jonas proposes a new imperative, expanding the Kantian categorical imperative. In his proposal, Jonas points out the need to

"to act in such a way that the effects of our action are compatible with the permanence of authentic human life on Earth" (3) (p.47). This would be the culmination of his thesis on the principle of responsibility.

The fascination aroused in the 19th century by the applications of science was followed by a 20th century alarmed by its applications in the military field, which radically altered the relationship between life and death in the world. The perversions of technology were sensed during the First World War, which had the effect of demystifying the scientist's mentality and revealing the ambivalence of technology. If the first alarm bells went off in 1914, the Second World War confirmed the true face of the catastrophe. The bombs on Hiroshima and Nagasaki and the deaths in the gas chambers attested to the unbridled power of man, with unpredictable consequences. Knowledge led to power, and the power to alter the environment and cause destruction led to new dimensions of order and disorder (10, 7). It was in witnessing these tragic events caused by man that Hans Jonas developed his principle of responsibility. Santos describes the building blocks of technoscience:

Modern technology has three main characteristics: technicality, globality and the potential for destruction. The first characteristic is not a redundancy, but is understood in the sense of its progressively autonomous basis allied to science. Globality refers to the universal reach of the effects; and finally, the potential for destruction is equated with the capacity for innovation and global reach (1) (p.135).

In this context, the last two characteristics should raise alarm bells about the way scientific knowledge is used, which once again legitimizes the importance of the Jonahian principle of responsibility, especially the heuristic of fear.

In addition to the behavior of scientists, we also have the fact that the acceleration of change and the pace of life are increasingly contributing to an attitude of discarding the future in favor of the present. This immediacy of living for the here and now, and the hypnotic state caused by the magic of technology, inhibit and dispense contemporary man from worrying about the distant future. Hans Jonas condemns this perspective when he states that *"the sacrifice of the future for the sake of the present is no more logically refutable than the sacrifice of the present for the sake of the future"* (3) (p.47). For the German philosopher, this non-reciprocal responsibility towards future generations is akin to parents caring for their children, which ensures the existence of offspring, and therefore of humanity.

And like all human action, technological progress undoubtedly has moral implications. We can therefore ask ourselves: what are we doing with our knowledge? From this perspective, the principle of responsibility proposed by Jonas aims, on the one hand, to contribute to a reformulation of the ethical and philosophical analysis of human action. On the other hand, it calls for a new form of education, aimed at curbing the human thirst for domination and ensuring a dignified life for humans and non-humans, within a preserved biosphere (1). The need for this new assessment is due to the fact that technological progress has not been associated with human moral progress; on the contrary, the dilapidation of the natural heritage and the emergence of many scientific innovations, positive in themselves, have had the reverse effect of degrading the human condition (10). This degradation is revealed in man's disconnection from nature, considering himself alien and superior to it, as well as seeing the natural environment merely as a reservoir of materials to meet his needs, without any concern for the carrying capacity of the resources exploited.

It was in this context that Jonas observed, throughout his work, that the way man views nature has been changing rapidly. In the beginning, action on it didn't cause much damage, because demand was limited and technoscience was more contemplative and analytical than interventional. However, the risk has increased with the rise of modern technology.

Jonas' PR also draws attention to the inadequacy of traditional ethical imperatives in the face of the new dimensions of collective action. Santos considers that *'Jonas's postulates are heirs to Kant's ethics, in the sense that they seek to establish an idea of duty. The fundamental difference is that, for Jonas, responsibility is centered on an asymmetrical and non-reciprocal relationship of care'* (1) (p.134), as well as referring to collective, public and social behavior (10). This idea is made explicit in the excerpt from the PR:

It is clear that our imperative focuses much more on public policy than on private conduct, the latter not being the causal dimension in which we can apply it. Kant's categorical imperative was aimed at the individual, and his criterion was momentary (3) (p.48).

In addition, Jonas considers Kant to be merely logical, formal, and unable to cope with the new reality of contemporaneity. He also criticizes the construction of the Kantian concept of morality, which states: *'in matters of morality, human reason can easily achieve a high degree of accuracy and perfection even among the simplest minds'* (3) (p.36). On this subject, Jonas points out that *'no other theorist of ethics has gone so far in diminishing the cognitive side of moral action'* (3) (p.37).

Some authors identify similarities between Jonah's assumptions and utilitarianism, which is refuted by Santos when he states that:

From the perspective of an emphasis on the final effects of action in the future, the ethics of responsibility could mistakenly be considered utilitarian, in the sense that the consequences produced by actions define whether they are morally good or bad. However, his ethics departs from classical utilitarianism in that it is not just a question of calculating the final effects of actions. Furthermore, he refers to unpredictable and incalculable effects, which eliminates any possibility of anticipation (1) (p.134).

We therefore agree with the authors who consider Hans Jonas' 'The Responsibility Principle' to be *'highly complex, in the sense that it touches on all fields of human action: science and technology, ecology, politics and education'* (10) (p.39). The German philosopher began constructing this theory at the beginning of the 1970s, but it is extremely topical in the sense that man is still dealing with the uncertainties and dangers generated by the application of science and technology. Recent examples of the harmful consequences of anthropogenic activity appear frequently in the national and international news. Unfortunately, it's not for lack of bad forecasts and the alarms that nature reveals that man no longer pursues the ideal of unlimited consumption, without considering that we live on a planet with finite resources. For this reason, the discussion of responsible behavior is becoming topical and indispensable.

4.2   WHO CARES ABOUT PRESERVING THE PLANET?

Environmental issues have received increasing attention, in the sense that the crisis is affecting the entire globe, without respect for geographical, political or economic boundaries. In this context, when in 2007 the Nobel Peace Prize was awarded to Al Gore and the International Panel on Climate Change, it became clear that the discussion about human action and nature is a relevant topic that deserves the most urgent attention.

The phenomenon of globalization has demanded a broadening of concepts related to human ethics, reviving the importance of other fields such as environmental ethics and animal ethics, both based on the principles of responsibility, precaution, sustainability and care (22). In all these principles, we recognize the ideas of Jonah about how man should behave in an increasingly technological world, with more and more threats to be avoided or managed.

The worsening of the planet's environmental problems and the progressive depletion of natural resources gave rise to the notion of sustainable development, which encompasses economic, social, technological and environmental issues. This concept emerged in 1983 with the drafting of the Brundtland Report, which warned of the need for all countries to admit that ecosystems are limited and that human action is reflected in their deterioration. Currently, the concept of sustainable development reveals an interconnection between the economy, the environment and society, in the sense that it advocates development that allows the needs of the present to be met without compromising the ability of future generations to live a dignified life. In this context, Fernandes points out that environmental education is one of the bases for education on a planetary scale, with the construction of new values adapted to contemporary problems (10). The concept of sustainable development has the Jonasian imperative at its core, insofar as it advocates that future generations be protected from damage caused by current anthropic activities.

This urgent need to change values requires building a new relationship with the other beings that inhabit the planet, by understanding that nature has an intrinsic value, and not just an instrumental one (17). Not to mention that the dependence between humanity and nature is indisputable, which leads us to conclude that the function of human intelligence will be to shape its organization in a way that is more harmonious with biological imperatives, changing patterns of behaviour based on prudence and responsibility.

Concern about the human being in a dignified world is also present in various religious segments, in which their representatives have increasingly called on their followers, rulers and people in general to reflect on their consumption habits and the way they see the world (2). For example,

Although Pope Francis does not explicitly cite Hans Jonas' PR in his 2015 Encyclical, there is an approximation throughout the document, insofar as both the philosopher and the Pontiff understand that the environmental crisis we are experiencing cannot be understood in isolation from other crises, be they of an ethical, political, human or social nature (25) (p.193).

In this way, the duty to future generations is a duty of humanity, including the public man and the ordinary citizen, and Jonas emphasizes that the more we sense the danger of the future, the more we must act in the present. This concern has been shared by other authors and opinion formers in the political, economic and educational fields, and is gradually sensitizing ordinary citizens to re-evaluate their particular actions in order to maintain a habitable planet for posterity.

4.3 REFLECTIONS OF JONASIAN THOUGHT

As we have already noted, we have identified Jonah's thoughts in areas of thought that directly interfere in everyday life. One of these is applied ethics, known as bioethics. This science is responsible for analyzing human relationships in various aspects, including dependencies with other species and with the environment, always seeking an ethical form in this relationship. Thus, one of the reasons that gave rise to bioethics was the increase in technology, which ultimately affects all living beings and nature (20). Hans Jonas' foundations permeate all of global bioethics, environmental ethics and the foundations of environmental education, in the sense of pursuing a new human conduct in the world. That's why we agree with Lecaros when he says that Potter's global bioethics addresses issues that are relevant from the time the term bioethics was coined until the present day, including: *'the danger of the development of technoscience, human progress and the survival of humanity, the moral obligation to the future, the control of technology, the need for an effort to achieve plural solutions to the ethical problems that arise in the clinical, biomedical and biotechnological spheres'* (22) (p.8).

More recent bioethical schools, such as the bioethics of intervention that has emerged in Latin America in recent decades, affirm that categories such as responsibility, care, precaution (in the face of the unknown) and prudence (in relation to advances and novelties) are indispensable for practicing bioethics with the environmental and planetary balance of the 21st century in mind. These ideas clearly show that they have taken on Hans Jonas' assumptions as the guiding principles of their philosophical construct (28).

Theologian Leo Pessini, at the opening of the 1st International Ibero-American Bioethics Congress in Curitiba (Brazil) in 2016, at which the Portuguese version of Van Rensselaer Potter's work 'Bioethics, a bridge to the future' was released, said that: humility, responsibility and competence are the foundations of Potterian bioethics. He also pointed out that the doctor's ideas were visionary and misunderstood by academics and scientists at the time the work was published. This misunderstanding was shared by Hans Jonas and his heuristic of fear, one of the main points of his work. Jonas gives fear an important role in his philosophical reflection, but it is fear that makes up responsibility, not fear that discourages action, but fear that drives the subject to consider the consequences of actions, building a more appropriate and careful behavior (1, 9, 5). This proposition about fear is nothing more than distrust of the way scientific knowledge is used. As already mentioned, the event of dangerous knowledge and the slippery slope is widely known in the academic and scientific world, and is defended by some scientists and technicians, which already legitimizes precaution. This is why we stress that it is the *apocalyptic and catastrophic nature of successful technology' that we should reflect on. Instead of remaining in the secure and illusory position of those who control the power of technology, we need to create a posture of reverence and fear'* (1) (p.137). Reverence would be for the power of scientific knowledge itself, and fear, in turn, would be related to the application of this knowledge, how it would be used and what the consequences would be. This is the theme of Hans Jonas' heuristic of fear, which makes it clear that "in the face of *imminent threats, the effects of which may yet reach us, fear is often the best substitute for true virtue and wisdom"* (3) (p.65).

In the same line of reasoning, we understand that the closer to the future that which is to be feared is, the more the heuristic of fear becomes necessary, because fear is a way of slowing down the speed of unlimited scientific knowledge, and can be the warning to bring us back to reason (5, 1).

Despite being strongly criticized by some authors, the heuristic of fear gave rise to one of the pillars of environmental law, which is the precautionary principle. This concept has spread to all legal instruments related to environmental issues, so that anthropogenic actions don't have such an impact on nature, as well as suggesting compensation mechanisms for environmental damage. The precautionary principle emerged with the Declaration of the Rio 92 Conference and states that: *'where there is a threat of serious or irremediable damage, the lack of full scientific certainty cannot be used as a reason for postponing cost-effective measures to prevent environmental degradation'* (21) (p.49). This principle is proactive rather than reactive, in the sense that it is applied when there is a possibility of a problem or damage, rather than reacting to a problem that has already occurred, and has proved to be an important tool in environmental science and environmental law (12). The precautionary principle is also present in international treaties, such as the Maastricht Treaty (which gave rise to the European Union), in which scientific uncertainty cannot be argued for actions that could have harmful consequences for the environment (10).

From an individual point of view, after a time of irrational confidence in human progress and capabilities, a part of society is entering a stage of greater awareness. There is a growing sensitivity towards the environment and caring for nature, and a sincere concern about what might happen to the planet (2). This concern is giving rise to a new way of thinking, which could be called environmental philosophy. This science has as its main object the ecological crisis and the analysis of morality, contained in the question *'does man have moral links with the environment, non-human species and ecosystems?'* (13) (p.76). Although the PR is focused on

However, we must not overlook the fact that one-off actions are of great importance in the sense that, as well as having an effect on the environment (even on a small scale), they have the power to raise awareness among other people, who in turn come together in groups and associations that can build alternative methods to solve local environmental problems.

In order to build paradigms that protect the natural environment from human activities, a new model of action was proposed at the Rio 92 Earth Conference, known as the 3R principle. Each of the 3Rs sets out a course of action to be followed in order to optimize man's presence in the environment and make it less aggressive. Reduce, recycle and reuse are the principles to be followed. Reduction is applied to both products and consumption, such as electricity, water or non-renewable fuels. The principle of recycling has been the most widely adopted today, as it brings various economic benefits to companies when they transform what would otherwise be waste into usable material. Finally, reuse seeks to give a product a new use, keeping it out of the non-biodegradable waste chain for as long as possible (21).

Several authors identify other principles that could be added to this list, such as the actions of rethinking, restructuring and refusing. Rethinking would be linked to evaluating what we really need in our way of life. The attitude of restructuring would be a consequence of the previous principle, as we would exchange the greed of individual well-being for the care of an entire group, taking into account the social and economic costs in the final calculation of consumer goods. And as a consequential action of the desired change in behavior, we would refuse all products that are superfluous to human existence (21). For us, this set of proposals clearly reflects Hans Jonas' principle of responsibility, which calls for a change in paradigms and behaviors, prioritizing the qualitative part of living over the quantitative portion.

The importance of the principle of responsibility is so topical because it evokes the need to preserve the good, the being, in short, the value that would protect man from the desire to instrumentalize and dominate the other, imposing on him the practice of efficiency and conservation as a new imperative, since the fear of annihilation and the call of the being make him aware of his obligation. In this way, the principle of responsibility proposed by Jonas is a rational one, aimed at collective action for the public good, capable of providing a critical and reflective dialogue in the midst of the technological age. As the first duty of the ethics of the future is to glimpse the long-term effects of our actions, it is necessary to think not only about the consequences of technology, but also about those arising from any form of human action, and not only for the present, but fundamentally for the future. (1, 10, 5).

The ethics of responsibility is also the foundation and purpose of education. This is because responsibility rests on the recognition of oneself and one's neighbor, and thus highlights the relationship between entities, making the educational process an ethical relationship. Purpose because responsibility calls for freedom, forcing a conscious decision to accept the other as a subject with rights, possibly without duties and in need of protection. On the other hand, *'if responsibility is not accepted as the purpose of education, knowledge will be lost,*

techniques and skills acquired by students can serve destruction, injustice, in short, ethical indifference" (10) (p.19). Also in relation to the educational process, but with a focus on the responsibility of teachers, Capo identifies the relevance of education when he suggests that *'educational professionals cannot hide behind technology and economics, but must share responsibility in the face of ethical dilemmas or seek to confront the long-term consequences of techno-scientific use'* (21) (p.48). This

he discussion must be plural, with different perspectives, always seeking to raise awareness of the importance of preserving our common home.

Still in the political-pedagogical sphere, the Belgrade Charter was a document drawn up by twenty environmental education experts during the UNEP/UNESCO Colloquium on Environmental Education in 1975. It places Jonas' principle of responsibility at the heart of its objectives, the clearest of which are: *"the development of responsible attitudes towards the environment and its protection; acquiring habits and customs that are in keeping with a careful appropriation of the resources of everyday use"* (21) (p.51).

4.4 TECHNOPHOBIA OR CAUTION?

In his Principle of Responsibility, Jonas makes it clear that he is not blaming either technology or science for the environmental catastrophes that are occurring and that are yet to come, but rather blames the Baconian program (of dominating and modifying nature through techno-science) for the crisis that has arisen, and also recognizes that capitalism has further exacerbated the problem, in the sense that it stimulates consumption in an unbridled and irresponsible way. Jonas advocates a measured and prudent use of science and technology, not their elimination (10:9).

With regard to the classification of Hans Jonas as a technophobe, we question whether warning about the consequences of a certain behavior would be the same as rejecting it completely. We don't think so, because we understand that this care ends up optimizing the management of the use of knowledge, trying to prevent possible harmful consequences, rather than advocating the denial of this knowledge.

Throughout his work, Jonas starts from the principle that technology is never neutral, that is, its application will generate consequences, whether they are expected or not. In this way, the thinker becomes a determined critic of the use of techno-scientific knowledge, especially in terms of 'limits of use', but he does not preach the renunciation of techno-scientific knowledge. For this reason, we don't consider Hans Jonas to be a technophobe, since the act of criticizing something doesn't mean aversion to the object of criticism.

The Belgian philosopher Gilbert Hottois created a new concept for the word technophobia, not respecting its etymological construction, as well as creating a classification of pejorative dubiousness, in which he inserts Hans Jonas. Furthermore, Jonas's criticism of the way technology is applied by man cannot culminate in his classification as a technophobe, since his work does not contain a *'sick fear or aversion to technology, but rather an informed perception of the situation and the need to recognize our responsibility with regard to future generations and the biosphere as a whole"* (9) (p.477), seeking to rationalize the use of technology.

Another point to note is that those who classify Jonas as a technophobe disregard the first term of the Jonasian concept 'heuristics of fear'. Heuristics means a method or process created with the aim of finding solutions to a problem, in other words, it is a methodology, a path to follow. In this way, the heuristic of fear can be understood as a way of considering the negative possibilities of an action, strictly speaking, considering its consequences. In other words, it would be a prudential appeal, because without it we wouldn't know how to act responsibly if we couldn't shudder in the face of some possibilities.

And on the relevance of scientific knowledge, Jonas states that *'the researcher must fully recognize the autonomy of his thinking activity, otherwise he can have no hope of obtaining the truth, nor of distinguishing between truth and non-truth, nor can he credit his thinking with any validity'* (3) (p.135).

Potter also understands the need for scientific knowledge and the limitations of its use when he states that it is necessary to *'foresee the consequences implicit in the application of new knowledge and to take more vigorous political action in the control of technology, while at the same time preserving its magnificent potential'* (7) (p.97).

In the course of this work, we have presented the concepts of dangerous knowledge and slippery slopes, demonstrating that in the scientific field there are researchers who consider their studies and objectives to be above good and evil, in other words, they understand that the search for and application of knowledge should be encouraged, without considering the possibility of harmful consequences and misuse. Now, if scientists have this conception that there are no barriers to scientific knowledge, there is no question of the need for ethical and moral limits to its application, since the results can be absolutely contrary to what is expected, as well as the possibility of them proving to be harmful and with even irreversible consequences. Hans Jonas had already foreseen this scenario when he emphasized that *'the mixture of beneficial and dangerous possibilities is clear, but the limits are not easy to swallow'* (3) (p.60).

To try to avoid the threat of the slippery slope, Warnock advocates a strictly legal limitation, i.e. through legislative instruments (23). But it is notorious that the advance of science is not accompanied by legal norms, a fact that leads to various conflicting situations created by science and which have no legal regulation, such as the use of embryonic stem cells for health treatments.

Still on the subject of Jonah's criticism of the use of technology, we disagree with Azambuja, who considers this idea obsolete, claiming that contemporary science is concerned with objects and objectives that are different from those of modern science. However, what techno-scientific application would be free of errors or unwanted consequences? Scientific evolution has not abolished the threats involved in its creation and application process. That would be both foolhardy and naïve. Can the technological order replace the natural order? Jonas clearly answers no. *'The order of technoscience has already revealed its failure to resolve natural, economic and social imbalances'* (10) (p.133).

These positions once again reinforce the urgency of discussions based on the principle of responsibility, which calls for reflection on human actions involving the use of technoscience. Jonah's critique of technology is one of the central aspects in the formulation of his proposal, but it is not a *'pessimistic view or a mere satanization of technology, but rather the realization of its real destructive power, which accompanies it like a shadow"* (1) (p.131). Therefore, being responsible requires us to cultivate a fear of the future that we can produce, in order to inspire prudence in our present actions, since what holds the worst danger also holds the best hope: the human mind itself (14:4).

4.5 THE IMPORTANCE OF COLLECTIVE AND INDIVIDUAL ACTION

Humanity has entered a new era in which the power of technology is bringing us to a crossroads. We are heirs to two centuries of enormous change, and it is only right that we should be proud of them and praise the efforts of scientists and technicians in the search for measures and instruments that make human life more comfortable. In this sense, well-directed techno-science can produce really valuable things to improve the quality of life of human beings (2).

On the other hand, it is notorious that not all actions with laudable objectives are carried out ethically, much less do they achieve their ends in the best way. There are countless examples of public and private projects that have culminated in catastrophes of exponential magnitude. If the heuristic of fear, revealed as the precautionary principle, had been respected, some of these damaging events could certainly have been avoided. *'Technological decisions should not be made on the basis of profit alone, but should be examined in terms of survival. This is where ecology and economics must meet, based on plural analysis to find possible solutions'* (7) (p.183). Problems such as biodiversity loss, biopiracy and climate change are of a global nature, as they are not geographically delimited. On the contrary, they are interconnected and far-reaching in time. Most environmental problems affect the whole of humanity and exacerbate situations of poverty, social vulnerability, food insecurity and the spread of diseases, among other social and political ills. Given the broad scope of environmental issues, they require discussions with all the players involved, in the search for collective solutions (22).

An emblematic example of augurs that proved harmful to nature and to man himself was the Green Revolution, which promised to alleviate planetary hunger by bombarding large plantations of a single species with gigantic quantities of pesticides. The aim was to maximize production, however, the homogeneity of the plantations was an easy target for specialist pathogens and pests, and the pesticides were concentrated in water sources and other organisms that would serve as food, increasing contamination. Can we say that scientists and government institutions were unaware of the possibility of these events? We believe that this is very unlikely. What seems more likely to us is that these possibilities were disregarded in favor of immediate results aimed ultimately at economic growth.

In this respect, *'politics and economics tend to blame each other for environmental degradation'* (2) (p.61), but the truth is that every system, whether political or economic, perpetuates itself as it prospers, even if it has no ethical guidelines (11). Today, most of the world is dominated by capitalism, which has already proven to be highly damaging to the natural environment with its paradigms of unbridled consumption and economic growth as its primary goal.

A reordering of regional, national and global priorities is therefore necessary. Policies to maximize economic growth, including environmental policy itself, need a quick and thorough reflection, involving the consequences of actions with regard to the management of available resources (29) (p.8).

But then it's time to ask ourselves: what would be the model capable of supplanting the dominant utilitarian model, in which economic growth and social welfare are based on the intensive use of resources and disrespect for nature's carrying capacity?

(10). Jonas states that *'Never before has public policy had to deal with issues of such scope and requiring such long time frames. In fact, the changed nature of human action alters the fundamental nature of politics'''* (3) (p.44).

In order to adapt to these changes in human nature, the foundations of economic growth need to be re-evaluated, in the sense that they only consider material values. The paradigm shift would be to include factors related to quality of life in the list to be evaluated, with the aim of recovering the human-nature relationship. Along these lines, the theory of economic degrowth demonstrates this concern, respecting the carrying capacity of natural resources and building new consumer values.

Undoubtedly, the concept of degrowth, introducing the finiteness of the planet and the slogan 'living better with less', has a number of undeniable virtues and, from a political perspective, can provide key elements for the future such as: the re-evaluation of terms like development, work or wealth, a deepening and rescue of social justice, citizenship and democracy, as well as the value of coherence between individual behavior and collective action (11) (p.22).

It must be emphasized that not only do political and public actions have weight and value, in other words, they must be imbued with the principle of responsibility; but specific actions are also extremely valuable for building new paradigms and social demands. An increasing number of people and social movements are beginning to use degrowth politics not only to live according to their ethical principles of responsibility, but also to organize, reflect on and present concrete proposals for change. Following this line of thought, ecological culture cannot be reduced to a set of urgent and partial solutions to the problems of environmental degradation that arise from human activity. It must be the basis for a different way of looking at things, a way of thinking, a policy, an educational program, a new perspective on behavior, which opposes the problems of environmental degradation.

resisting the advance of the technocratic paradigm (2, 11)

In Jonah's work, he makes it clear that his proposals are aimed more at

However, it is undeniable how important it is for everyone to change their behavior with regard to issues such as the treatment of household waste, the disposal of oily substances and water consumption, for the future of the planet and those to come. On this point, we agree with Fernandes when he states that:

When Jonas imposes the principle of responsibility on governmental power, or on intellectual elites, he confers a certain alienation on ordinary citizens with regard to their individual daily responsibilities. This was one of the points of his philosophy that was widely criticized. In practice, elites can often represent organized interests that run counter to the dignity of life. Ordinary people, through non-corporate organizations, can dismantle less clear interests by promoting debates that generate controversy and extreme positions, thus bringing camouflaged intentions to light (10) (p.83).

In the same vein, Hannah Arendt also believed in the importance of individual actions when she disagreed with the *cog-theory,* which attributes to all the participants in a system the simple condition of being the handles of a *cog,* and that they would therefore have no individual responsibility for the whole set of actions.

Arendt's reflection becomes pertinent in the sense that the fundamental problems of modern society consist precisely in the lack of political organization and the unthinking use of technological advances, because people no longer exercise the power to think critically, they are simply led to passively assume and repeat behaviors (18) (p.398).

It is these paradigms that need to be changed, since justice towards others and a possible future is not translated as benevolence, empathy or care, but as responsibility.

4.6   WHY SHOULD WE ACT RESPONSIBLY?

Despite our big cities and the technological advances that have intervened in our lives, we still continue to live on planet Earth, in the midst of nature and dependent on it. Reflection on the uncertainty of future life is the result of a mistake made in isolating human beings from the rest of nature, which generates a mixture of feelings of guilt, frustration and a defensive attitude in various segments of the population, when there should be a unified attempt to achieve the social wisdom that will allow humanity to survive and improve the quality of life (7, 5). Hans Jonas stated in his work that, in order for humanity to consider changing its paradigms, it is necessary for one to see the other (including the unborn) and nature with a new value, which he conceptualizes as:

a designation of the magnitude of the will, how much one wants to invest, and not a duty. I establish something as my purpose because it is valuable to me, or something is valuable to me because my needy nature has established it as my purpose, before any choice is made. In acting, insofar as it is free from competing purposes, I again impose the purpose of nature as my purpose. Thus, any goal that I impose on myself becomes valuable by this simple fact, insofar as I consider it worth pursuing (including the renunciation of all those goals that are not compatible with this goal) (3) (p.154155).

Still on the subject of building values and raising human awareness, he states that:

For something to reach me and affect me in a way that influences my will, I need to be able to be influenced by it. Our emotional side has to come into play. And it is in the very essence of our moral nature that our intellect conveys to us an appeal that finds a response in our feeling. It is the feeling of responsibility. If we were not receptive to the appeal of duty in emotional terms, even the most rigorous and rationally impeccable demonstration of its correctness would be powerless to produce a motivating force (3) (p.157).

In fact, for something to have value for me, I have to be touched by it, I have to understand its relevance and my dependence on it. In this context, humanity is beginning to respond to nature's call to act responsibly in all its actions, even the most mundane. This new appreciation of the natural environment gives rise to new social demands, i.e. communities begin to demand more green areas from the authorities, more organic food, better treatment of animals, among other things.

All the necessary behavioral changes (individual and collective) are perfectly achievable, because men are potential moral beings because they have the capacity to be sensitized. In the same way, *'fighting, caring, respecting, renouncing, and above all, acting responsibly, is an essentially ethical act, and one that is within our power"* (5) (p.84).

Furthermore, changing paradigms regarding consumption and small human activities (without devaluing government actions) is a matter of survival, given that many of the consequences of the inappropriate use of technology are far-reaching and immediate. In this sense, Potter was already warning that: *'the survival of world civilization will be impossible unless there is some agreement on a system of common values, especially on the concept of an obligation to future generations'* (7) (p.205).

5. FINAL CONSIDERATIONS

Hans Jonas is considered one of the leading contemporary philosophers due to his concern about human actions and their consequences for the environment and future generations. He considered that future generations could not be held hostage to the irresponsible acts of those already on the planet, who would leave behind an earth devastated by environmental disasters, loss of biodiversity and other consequences due to the inadvertent use of technology developed by science.

Jonas focuses on the future dimension of human action, proposing a dialog between philosophy and the sciences, taking up the reflection on the future. His thesis stems from his concern about the future and its long-term effects, since it is the uses to which knowledge is put that can make it dangerous. When he criticizes traditional ethics, he doesn't intend to replace or eliminate it, but rather to complement it with the principle of responsibility. Such an intention would aim to update ethical analysis in the face of the modernization of technology and the new human action, which requires more tools and considerations than traditional ethics offers.

Another key point in Jonah's work is the proposition of the heuristic of fear, which we have identified in areas related to philosophy, such as the construction of legal instruments aimed at the environment, in the form of the precautionary principle. This principle seeks to warn about the possible undesirable consequences of using scientific knowledge and is used as a guide in many environmental laws around the world.

Hans Jonas' thinking also reverberates in education, as it transforms people into conscious citizens who are committed to the community and the environment that surrounds them; in the economy, in the sense that new ways of evaluating material goods are already being introduced, valuing those that are more closely linked to quality of life; and in politics, which is increasingly seeking to create management tools that meet new social demands. These demands are present to the extent that man understands that the maintenance of nature is a condition for human survival, and it is in the context of this destiny that Jonas preaches the dignity of nature, the urgency of a new construct of the human-nature relationship.

Nature, the support and condition of humanity, past and present, is constitutively vulnerable. If it is currently at risk, it is up to man, who shares this vulnerability, to take responsibility for its preservation, since he has made it a thing through the recklessness of his unbridled power and ambition. We must therefore consider the impossibility of infinite growth in a finite world, in other words: humanity must become aware of the need to change its lifestyle, production and consumption. In the same way, it is necessary for the techno-scientific community to act with the utmost caution when using technology.

We don't preach renouncing or abandoning technoscience. On the contrary, we encourage the search for technical alternatives that use natural resources with greater responsibility and respect for recovery time. Furthermore, we recognize the need for scientific knowledge and its application to remedy the damage caused to nature by human technology itself. We therefore believe that this was the main idea of Hans Jonas, who, despite being misunderstood by some and classified as a technophobe by others, has had his importance recognized to the extent that his assumptions are reflected in areas that directly influence human life.

In this way, calls for responsibility must grow in proportion to the achievements of power. No one wants to return to the Stone Age, but it is essential to slow down in order to look at reality in a different way, to take advantage of the positive and sustainable advances and, at the same time, to recover the values and the great goals. We can't deny this world, much less run away from it, but we must build a new one from what we have available today and use as a basis a proposal of ethical responsibility based on respect for the consequences of actions for future generations.

Despite human arrogance and selfishness, we are also capable of caring for and cooperating on behalf of those who are vulnerable in some way, be they humans, animals or even the environment. For the formation of this new awareness, Hans Jonas' principle of responsibility appears as a key element, since it advocates a new ethical imperative to be pursued, namely: 'act in such a way that your actions are not harmful to your natural environment or to future generations'.

BIBLIOGRAPHICAL REFERENCES

Santos R. The problem of technology and the critique of translation in Hans Jonas' ethics.

Revista Bioethikos 2011; 5(2): 130-140. Available at:www.saocamilo-sp.**br/pdf/bioethikos/85/130-140.**pd. Accessed on 27/11/2016.

Francis P. Encyclical Letter *Laudato si:* on the care of our common home. Vatican City. 2015.

Jonas H. O Principio Responsabilidade, ensaio de uma ética para a civilizaçao tecnologica. 2.ed. Rio de Janeiro, Brazil: Contraponto Editora LTDA; 2006.

Azambuja CC. Ethics and technoscience. Revista de Filosofia Aurora 2013; 25(36): 323-340.

Battestin C, Ghiggi G. Hans Jonas' principle of responsibility: an ethical principle for the new times. Revista Thaumazein 2010; 3(6): 69-85. Available at: http://sites.unifra.br/thaumazein. Accessed on: 10/10/2016.

Morin E. Para sair do seculo XX. Rio de Janeiro: Editora Nova Fronteira; 1986.

Potter VR. Bioethics, a bridge to the future. Sao Paulo: Loyola; 2016.

Goya W. The principle of responsibility-Hans Jonas, Reviews of a classic. Available at:http://www.filosofia.com.br/vi classic.php7idM8. Accessed on 20/10/2016.

Fonseca LSG. Does Hans Jonas blame technology for the current environmental crisis?

Journal of Philosophy Aurora 2012; 24(35): 465-480. Available at: www2.pucpr.br/reol/index.php/rf?dd99=pdf&dd1=7514. Accessed on 2/10/2016

Fernades, MFA. Hans Jonas' principle of responsibility. In search of ethical foundations for contemporary education [Dissertation]. Porto: Faculty of Letters of the University of Porto; 2002. Available at: https://repositorio-aberto.up.pt/.../N6023TM01PFATIMAFERNANDES000068709. Accessed on 29/10/2016.

Cabral ES, Xavier BHR. Overcoming the current model of sustainable development from the perspective of Hans Jonas and Latouche's policy of degrowth. *In:* Proceedings of the VII Congress of Humanization and Bioethics/ I Iberoamerican Congress of Bioethics, 2016; Curitiba: Pontificia Universidade Catolica. Produgoes Editoriais Catalina, p. 17-24.

Botkin DB, Keller EA. Environmental science: Earth, a living planet. Rio de Janeiro: LTC Ltda; 2011.

13.Shramm RF. *Desconstruyendo el 'desarollo sustentable' y la alternativa de 'decrecimiento' en la era de la globalización.* Revista Redbioetica/UNESCO 2015; 6(1): 70-79. Available at: www.unesco.org/new/fileadmin/MULTIMEDIA/.../Bioet-RevistaBioetica-11-web.pdf Accessed on 5/11/2016.

Morin E. Os sete saberes necess necessárias a educagao do futuro. 2.ed. Sao Paulo, Brazil: Editora Cortez; 2000.

Capra F. Ecological literacy: the challenge for 21st century education. *In:* Trigueiro A (coord). Environment in the 21st century. Sao Paulo: Armazem do Ipe; 2008. p. 19-34.

Boff L. Ecology and spirituality. In: Trigueiro A (coord). Environment in the 21st century. Sao Paulo: Armazem do Ipe; 2008. p. 34-43.

Batista RS, Rogas G, Gomes AP, Minardi R, Cotta M, Messecer JC. Bioethics Are environmental and deep ecology paradigms for thinking about the 21st century? Revista Eletronica do Mestrado Profissional em Ensino de Ciencias da Saude e do Ambiente 2009; 2(1): 44-51. Available at: **ensinosaudeambiente**.uff.br/index.php/ensinosaudeambiente/article/download/ 41/41. Accessed on 5/11/2016.

18.Siqueira JE. Irreflection and the banality of evil in Hannah Arendt's thought. Revista Bioethikos 2011; 5(4): 392-400. Available at: www.saocamilo-sp.br/pdf/bioethikos/89/A5.pdf. Accessed on 14/11/2016.

19.Sirvinskas LP. Manual of Environmental Law. Sao Paulo: Saraiva; 2011.

Cortina A. *Bioethics for the 21st century: building hope.* Magazine

Iberoamericana de Bioetica 2016; 1: 1-12. Available at:

revistas.upcomillas.es/index.../bioetica-revista-iberoamericana/. Accessed on

5/12/2016.

Capo MA, Drane J. *Bioethical planning of the environment.* Magazine

Bioethikos 2014; 8(1): 46-52. Available at: www.saocamilo-

sp.br/pdf/bioethikos/155560/a3.pdf Accessed on 11/11/2016.

Lecaros JA. *Global bioethics and the ethics of responsibility: a phenomenological*

look at the origins and challenges for the future. Revista

Iberoamericana de Bioetica 2016; 1: 01-13. Available at:

https://revistas.upcomillas.es/.../bioetica-revista-iberoamericana.Accessed   on:

14/11/2016.

Warnock M. The human genome project: ethics and the law. *In:* The uses of

philosophy.

1 ed. Sao Paulo, Brazil. Papirus Editora. 1994.

Carson R. Silent Spring. 1.ed.Sao Paulo, Brazil: Ed. Gaia LTDA; 2012.

Beraldo RA. Approximations between Pope Francis' encyclical *Laudato Si'* and

Hans Jonas' The Principle of Responsibility. *In: Proceedings of* the VII Congress

of Humanization and Bioethics/ I Iberoamerican Congress of Bioethics, 2016;

Curitiba: Pontificia Universidade Catolica. Produgoes Editoriais Catalina, p. 193.

Nascimento EP. The trajectory of sustainability, from environmental to social, from

social to economic. Estudos Avangados 2012; 26 (74): 51-64. Available at:

file:///C:/Users/t315755/Downloads/10624-13471-1-PB%20(2).pdf.

Accessed

on: 15/12/2016.

Bocato-Franco AA. Understanding degrowth 2013. Available at:

http://www.cartacapital.com.br/blogs/outras-palavras/para-compreender-o-

201cdecrescimento201d-3687.html. Accessed on: 15/12/2016.

Garrafa V. From bioethics of principles to an interventional bioethics. Magazine

Bioetica 2005; 13(1): 125-134. Available at:

http: //www.revistabioetica.cfm.org.br/index.php/revista bioetica/article/viewF ile/97/102. Accessed on: 13/12/2016.

Peres JA. Bioethics and the environment. Available at:
http://repositorio.ucp.pt/bitstream/10400.14/4790/1/com-
inter 2008 IB 1609 araujo joana 06.pdf. Accessed on: 10/11/2016.

Printed by Books on Demand GmbH, Norderstedt / Germany